MW01703113

Specific Skill Series
for Language Arts

Research

Leveled Books in Nine Key Language Arts Skill Areas

SRA

Columbus, OH

The McGraw·Hill Companies

Cover: ©Tim Flach/Getty Images, Inc.

SRAonline.com

SRA

Send all inquiries to:
SRA/McGraw-Hill
4400 Easton Commons
Columbus, OH 43219

Printed in the United States of America.

ISBN 0-07-601709-5

4 5 6 7 8 9 RHR 12 11 10

TO THE TEACHER

GENERAL INFORMATION ON RESEARCH

The ability to ask questions and use an effective research process to find and present conclusions is a vital skill for students as they progress through school and in later life. In addition to traditional sources, the Internet has provided society with an overload of information. The task of today's student is to find appropriate information and use it to answer questions and solve problems. Knowing how to find, summarize, and present information makes the difference between a good student and a poor student.

Teaching students how to conduct research can be divided into two groups: research skills and research processes. Research skills are related to gathering appropriate information. These include learning to use books and other print materials, charts, graphs, surveys, and the Internet. In the research process, students employ research skills. An effective research process includes getting ideas; asking appropriate questions; narrowing a topic and formulating a research statement; gathering, evaluating, and outlining information; taking notes; summarizing; drafting paragraphs; and writing a bibliography.

ABOUT *SPECIFIC SKILL SERIES FOR LANGUAGE ARTS*

Specific Skill Series for Language Arts is a companion to ***Specific Skill Series,*** a supplemental reading program that has been widely recognized for its effectiveness for over thirty years. The two series are designed and organized the same. ***Specific Skill Series for Language Arts*** consists of discrete units of practice exercises that target and reinforce fundamental language-arts skills. Units in both series are presented in multiple-choice format for standardized test practice.

ABOUT *RESEARCH*

The scope and sequence for Books A through H of *Research* focuses on research skills and processes. The scope and sequence for each book is located on the last page of the book. Each unit includes

- **rule boxes** that explain research skills and processes.
- **models** in each rule box to illustrate the skills and processes.
- **multiple-choice exercises** for skills practice and reinforcement.

Four **Language Activity Pages** (LAPs) appear in each book. Each LAP is divided into the following four sections and reviews the skills practiced in the preceding units:

Exercising Your Skill reviews key terms and concepts.

Expanding Your Skill provides mixed practice.

Exploring Language shows how the skills apply to real-world contexts by featuring one of six forms of writing: descriptive, narrative, personal, persuasive, expository, and poetry.

Expressing Yourself includes two creative activities related to the skills. One activity is always a Work-with-a-Partner activity to encourage collaborative learning.

TO THE TEACHER

SERIES COMPONENTS

- **Student Editions:** Nine books in each level (A–H) focus on nine skill areas: *Grammar, Usage, Mechanics, Spelling, Vocabulary, Sentences, Paragraphs, Writing Process,* and *Research.*
- **Placement Test Books:** One book for each skill area includes diagnostic tests to place students in the correct level.
- **Teacher's Manual:** Primarily an answer key, the *Teacher's Manual* also includes reproducible student worksheets and further information on how to use the program, including classroom management tips.

HOW TO USE *SPECIFIC SKILL SERIES FOR LANGUAGE ARTS*

Placing Students in Levels: The scope and sequence, complexity of skills, and readability in Levels A through H correspond to Grades 1 through 8. Students may, however, be placed in any level. For example, in the second grade, a student who needs remedial work in a specific skill may be placed in Book A, an on-level student who would benefit from skills reinforcement may be placed in Book B, and an advanced student who is ready for enrichment may be placed in Book C or higher. *Placement Tests* help place students in the correct level.

Setting: This series can be used for independent study and one-on-one practice sessions, as well as in small-group and whole-class settings. It is also effective in after-school and summer-school programs.

Getting Started: Students must have notebook paper or copies of reproducible student worksheets (located in the *Teacher's Manual*) before they begin working. Remind students not to write in the books. Students may begin in any unit of any book, depending on the skill practice they need, although it is recommended that they begin with Unit 1. As they work through the units, students should record their answers on notebook paper or on the student worksheets.

Pacing: Students should be encouraged to work at their own pace, completing a few units every day or every other day.

Scoring: Teachers should score units as soon as they have been completed. Then a discussion can be held in which students justify their answer choices.

Internet Use: Some activities, especially those in *Research,* require students to use the Internet. Students' use of the Internet should be monitored closely for content appropriateness and safety.

TO THE STUDENT

Research is asking questions about a topic and then finding the answers to those questions. To find the answers you need to know how to use different sources, including books, magazines, and the Internet. This book will show you how to research a topic.

In Book E *Research,* you will learn about

- Using a Table of Contents and an Index
- Using an Encyclopedia
- Finding Magazine and Newspaper Articles
- Key Word Searching
- Evaluating a Web Site
- Reading Graphs and Charts
- Getting Ideas and Narrowing Topics
- Formulating Questions
- Making a Research Statement
- Identifying Sources
- Comparing Information across Sources
- Taking Notes and Summarizing
- Writing an Outline
- Writing Introductory, Supporting, and Concluding Paragraphs
- Writing a Bibliography

After you complete this book, you will be able to use the information you find to write different kinds of reports. Many reports adapt information from graphs and charts; some reports actually include graphs and charts to share or summarize information. Knowing how to read, and sometimes interpret, the data on a graph or chart is important when researching.

Family Life			
Name	**Brothers?**	**Sisters?**	**Pets?**
Kyle	no	yes	yes
Chloe	no	no	yes
Clark	no	no	yes
Annette	yes	yes	no

By mastering the skills in this book, you will know more about using sources of information and writing an effective research report.

Unit 1
Using a Table of Contents and an Index

To do research, you need to know how to use resources to find information. You can use a **table of contents,** located in the front of a book, to find chapters and their page numbers. An **index,** located in the back of a book, can be used to find the exact page number for a topic. An index is in alphabetical order.

Use the table of contents below to answer the questions.

Caves

1. Chapter 2 contains information on all of the following *except*
   (A) rimstone pools. **(C)** bats.
   (B) columns. **(D)** stalactites and stalagmites.

2. Which chapter provides information on the people who currently live in caves?
   (A) Chapter 1 **(C)** Chapter 3
   (B) Chapter 2 **(D)** Chapter 4

3. Which chapter provides information on Mammoth Cave, a well-known cave in Kentucky?
   (A) Chapter 2 **(C)** Chapter 4
   (B) Chapter 3 **(D)** Chapter 5

4. Which chapter provides information about bats?
   (A) Chapter 2 **(C)** Chapter 4
   (B) Chapter 3 **(D)** Chapter 5

Unit 1

Using a Table of Contents and an Index

Use the index below to answer the questions.

Index

5. Which pages provide information about the Anasazi people?

(A) 27–30 **(C)** 37–38
(B) 35–37 **(D)** 40–41

6. According to the index, what type of cave-dwelling animal is an owl?

(A) a speleologist **(C)** a helictite
(B) a troglobite **(D)** a troglophile

7. Pages 42–52 provide information on all of the following *except*

(A) Stephen Bishop. **(C)** spelunkers.
(B) Neanderthals. **(D)** Éduoard-Alfred Martel.

8. According to the index, what is a *helictite?*

(A) a type of cave formation **(C)** a cave animal
(B) a soda straw **(D)** a speleologist

9. Which pages contain information about water tables?

(A) 20–21 **(C)** 7–10
(B) 2–4 **(D)** 31–32

10. Which pages contain information about amateur spelunkers?

(A) 45–46 **(C)** 42–44
(B) 49–52 **(D)** 47–49

Unit 2

Using an Encyclopedia

Encyclopedias contain collections of **entries** about a variety of **topics.** Each entry has general, factual information that is usually written by an expert. An encyclopedia is a good place to start your research because it will give you the basic information you need to know about your topic and provide you with key words to use in your search.

Complete each sentence below.

1. If you looked up *fuels* in an encyclopedia, you would *not* find information about
   (A) natural gas.
   (B) fossil fuels.
   (C) oil.
   (D) electricity.

2. If you looked up *flowers* in an encyclopedia, you would find information about
   (A) the parts of a flower.
   (B) how to plant a vegetable garden.
   (C) which flowers grow best in your yard.
   (D) trees.

3. If you looked up *Japan* in an encyclopedia, you would *not* find information about
   (A) the flag of Japan.
   (B) Japan's neighbor, South Korea.
   (C) the major cities in Japan.
   (D) the history of Japan.

4. If you looked up *rabbits* in an encyclopedia, you would *not* find information about
   (A) what rabbits eat.
   (B) the developmental cycle of rabbits.
   (C) whether a rabbit can outrun a fox.
   (D) the different types of rabbits.

5. If you looked up *tornado* in an encyclopedia, you would *not* find information about
(A) how tornadoes are formed.
(B) how to measure the severity of a tornado.
(C) where tornadoes commonly occur.
(D) how tornado effects are filmed for movies.

---

6. If you looked up *coins* in an encyclopedia, you would find information about
(A) the current Secretary of the Treasury of the United States.
(B) how much a Kennedy half dollar is currently worth.
(C) why people toss coins into fountains.
(D) what materials coins are made from.

---

7. If you looked up *Smithsonian Institution* in an encyclopedia, you would find information about
(A) Washington, D.C.
(B) who founded the Smithsonian Institution.
(C) the hours the Smithsonian Institution is open to the public.
(D) the most popular museums in the United States.

---

8. If you looked up *soccer* in an encyclopedia, you would *not* find information about
(A) the rules of soccer.
(B) the soccer leagues in your city.
(C) who invented soccer.
(D) what a penalty kick is.

---

9. If you looked up *diamonds* in an encyclopedia, you would find information about
(A) how diamonds are cut and polished.
(B) other things that are also formed by carbon.
(C) gold and silver.
(D) the phone number of a diamond jeweler.

---

10. If you looked up *citrus fruits* in an encyclopedia, you would *not* find information about
(A) where citrus fruits are grown.
(B) the nutritional value of citrus fruits.
(C) how to make lemonade.
(D) the varieties of citrus fruits.

Unit 3

Finding Magazine and Newspaper Articles

You can use a **periodicals index** to find magazine and newspaper articles about a topic. Many of these indexes are found on the Internet or in a library. A search of the index brings up a list of **citations.** A citation tells information about an article.

A citation often gives the following information:

the title of the article

the author of the article

the title of the magazine or newspaper in which the article appears

the volume number of the magazine or newspaper

the issue number of the magazine or newspaper

the page numbers of the article

the date the magazine or newspaper was published

ARTICLE TITLE — AUTHOR

How to Write Research Papers That Get *A*'s. I. Smarty.

Kid's Writing Quarterly v9 n17 p21-27 Jan. 2000

MAGAZINE TITLE — VOLUME NUMBER — ISSUE NUMBER — PAGE NUMBERS — DATE

Below is a list of citations from a periodicals index. Use the list to answer the questions.

SPACE TRAVEL

An Interview with an Astronaut. K. B. Blanks. *Space Age Times* v12 n8 p6-11 Apr. 7 1999

Manned Space Flights: Are They Still Worth the Risk? C. D. Stark. *Newsbeat* v16 n3 p19-24 Jan. 26 2003

New Technology Improves Shuttle Design. J. Riley. *Timely Magazine* v7 n36 p4-6 Aug. 9 1977

Shuttling to Mars—Will It Become a Reality? R. Sexton. *The Finkelstein Report* v3 n19 p12-16 July 14 2003

Space Travel and the Effects of Weightlessness on the Body. C. Strode. *Science Research Journal* v6 n22 p34-42 Oct. 29 1993

What's after Jupiter: The Next Steps for the Space Program. B. Brewer. *Children's Rocketship* v1 n10 p78-79 May 19 2001

1. In which month was "Shuttling to Mars—Will It Become a Reality?" published?
   (A) October
   (B) April
   (C) May
   (D) July

2. How many pages is the article "Space Travel and the Effects of Weightlessness on the Body"?
   (A) five
   (B) four
   (C) nine
   (D) cannot be determined from the information given

---

3. Which article is the most recent?
   (A) "Space Travel and the Effects of Weightlessness on the Body"
   (B) "New Technology Improves Shuttle Design"
   (C) "Shuttling to Mars—Will It Become a Reality?"
   (D) "Manned Space Flights: Are They Still Worth the Risk?"

---

4. Which article is the shortest?
   (A) "An Interview with an Astronaut"
   (B) "What's after Jupiter: The Next Steps for the Space Program"
   (C) "Shuttling to Mars—Will It Become a Reality?"
   (D) "Manned Space Flights: Are They Still Worth the Risk?"

---

5. Which article is most likely to have outdated information?
   (A) "New Technology Improves Shuttle Design"
   (B) "Manned Space Flights: Are They Still Worth the Risk?"
   (C) "Shuttling to Mars—Will It Become a Reality?"
   (D) "Space Travel and the Effects of Weightlessness on the Body"

---

6. Which article is most likely to give a personal point of view about space travel?
   (A) "Shuttling to Mars—Will It Become a Reality?"
   (B) "New Technology Improves Shuttle Design"
   (C) "An Interview with an Astronaut"
   (D) "What's after Jupiter: The Next Steps for the Space Program"

---

7. Which article was published in a scientific journal?
   (A) "Shuttling to Mars—Will It Become a Reality?"
   (B) "An Interview with an Astronaut"
   (C) "Space Travel and the Effects of Weightlessness on the Body"
   (D) "Manned Space Flights: Are They Still Worth the Risk?"

Unit 3

Finding Magazine and Newspaper Articles

Below is a list of citations from a periodicals index. Use the list to answer the questions.

ALASKA

A Brief History of the Iditarod Sled Race. D. Gilbert. *Competitor's Monthly* v27 n4 p19–27 Dec. 2003

Effects of Permafrost on Arctic Plant Life. A. X. Lang. *Plant Life Magazine* v 19 n53 p11–14 June 17 2003

How Cold Is It? What to Expect from an Alaskan Winter. N. Rathbun. *Curious Kid's Journal of Science and Nature* v4 n5 p2–7 Oct. 2001

Midnight Baseball Game Breaks Attendance Record. S. B. Lewis. *Candlewood Evening News* v76 n31 pA1

Ranger Captures Moose on Rooftop. M. Munson. *Nenana Bugle* v54 n18 pA2

Sleds, Skis, and Snowmachines: How We Get from Here to There. D. Keener and R. Cody. *Sporting Life for Kids* v7 n15 p7–12 Aug. 21 1995

Tracking a Family of Moose in Denali. C. McIntyre. *International Geographic Magazine for Kids* v63 n41 p91-95 Aug. 1998

What Are the Northern Lights? T. J. Bailey. *Kids Science Quarterly* v9 n88 p45–52 Mar. 2000

What's It Really Like Here? A Day with an Alaskan Sixth-Grader. N. Platt. *Children's Life* v11 n75 p10–16 Feb. 2003

Wonderland Castle Wins Ice-Carving Competition. L. Runck. *Ninilchik Morning Sun* v348 n97 pD1

---

8. Which of the following is *not* a newspaper article?
   (A) "Midnight Baseball Game Breaks Attendance Record"
   (B) "Tracking a Family of Moose in Denali"
   (C) "Ranger Captures Moose on Rooftop"
   (D) "Wonderland Castle Wins Ice-Carving Competition"

---

9. In which publication does the article about the baseball game appear?
   (A) *Competitor's Monthly*
   (B) *Plant Life Magazine*
   (C) *Candlewood Evening News*
   (D) *Ninilchik Morning Sun*

10. Which article is co-authored (written by more than one person)?
(A) "Sleds, Skis, and Snowmachines: How We Get from Here to There"
(B) "Effects of Permafrost on Arctic Plant Life"
(C) "A Brief History of the Iditarod Sled Race"
(D) "Tracking a Family of Moose in Denali"

---

11. In which month was the article about moose in Denali published?
(A) February
(B) June
(C) August
(D) December

---

12. On what page does the article about the moose on the rooftop begin?
(A) 91
(B) 52
(C) 18
(D) A2

---

13. In which month was the Iditarod article published?
(A) December
(B) March
(C) June
(D) August

---

14. Whose article might you use if you wanted to research how Alaskan children live?
(A) Platt
(B) Runck
(C) Gilbert
(D) Bailey

---

15. In which publication would you find the article about Alaska's weather?
(A) *International Geographic Magazine for Kids*
(B) *Curious Kid's Journal of Science and Nature*
(C) *Nenana Bugle*
(D) *Kid's Science Quarterly*

The First LAP
Language Activity Pages

A. Exercising Your Skill

You have been learning how to use resources such as tables of contents, indexes, and encyclopedias. You have also learned how to find magazine and newspaper articles in periodicals indexes. Answer the following questions about what you have learned.

1. An encyclopedia is a useful resource when researching a topic because
   (A) it includes citations of magazine and newspaper articles.
   (B) it provides an overview of all the chapters in a book.
   (C) it provides general factual information about a variety of topics.

2. An index is a useful resource when researching a topic because
   (A) it includes citations of magazine and newspaper articles.
   (B) it provides an overview of all the chapters in a book.
   (C) it lists exact page numbers for specific topics.

3. A periodicals index is a useful resource when researching a topic because
   (A) it includes citations of magazine and newspaper articles.
   (B) it provides general factual information about a variety of topics.
   (C) it lists exact page numbers for specific topics.

B. Expanding Your Skill

Number your paper from 1 to 2. Then choose the best resource to use to complete each task below.

1. You want to find the page number in your history book that tells where the country of Bosnia is located.
   (A) encyclopedia
   (B) table of contents
   (C) index

2. You want to find an article in the newspaper about what is currently happening in Bosnia.
   (A) periodicals index
   (B) table of contents
   (C) index

C. Exploring Language

Expository Writing Read the following paragraph. Then choose the resource that would best help the writer find more information.

Mineralogists identify minerals and conduct research to find ways for people to use them. They study the structure of minerals to see what the crystal structure is inside the mineral. Another duty of a mineralogist is to classify minerals and study their characteristics. They use special instruments to look inside the mineral and photograph the internal structure. Mineralogists also study physical properties of minerals, such as hardness, color, luster, and conductivity.

To find general information about minerals,

(A) look for the word *minerals* in the index of a science book.

(B) look in a periodicals index for newspaper articles about recent scientific discoveries.

(C) look in the table of contents of an American history book.

(D) look up the word *science* in an encyclopedia.

D. Expressing Yourself

Choose one of these activities. When you are finished, give your paper to your teacher.

1. Select a current topic to research, and go to the school or public library. Tell the librarian that you would like to use a periodicals index to find current articles about the topic you chose. Find one article from the list of citations. Then print or photocopy the article. Divide into groups in class, and share your findings. Tell your group what your topic is, and read your article's title, its source name, and its date of printing. Tell why or why not the article was a good source of information.

2. WORK with a PARTNER Choose a topic with your partner that you would both like to research, such as *the rain forest* or *cars of the future*. Find and read an entry about your topic in an encyclopedia. Then make a list of three questions that you still have after reading the entry. Finally, write a plan for finding the answers to your questions.

Unit 4
Key Word Searching

You can find information more easily on the Internet and in library databases if you use specific **key words.**

- If you are looking for information about baseball bats, you should key *baseball bats* in the search box. If you keyed only *bats*, you would get a list of Web sites about different kinds of bats, for example, mammals, not just baseball bats.
- To make your search even more specific, use quotation marks around the subject you key in the search box. By keying "*science fair projects,*" you can make sure you *only* get information about science fair projects. The search engine will search for Web sites that contain *only* the key words in the order in which you keyed them.
- You can also key the word AND between two words or phrases you are searching. If you key "*science fair projects*" AND *volcanoes,* you will get a list of Web sites about making a volcano as a science fair project.

Choose the best key words to find Web sites containing answers to each question below.

1. Why don't people fall out of roller coasters when they go upside-down?
   (A) "amusement park rides" AND physics
   (B) physics
   (C) roller coaster AND amusement park rides
   (D) ride AND park

---

2. How long does it take a forest to recover from a fire?
   (A) "forest fire" AND recovery
   (B) fire AND forest
   (C) recovery
   (D) forests AND safety

---

3. At what speed does the fastest bird fly?
   (A) "fly fastest" AND airplane
   (B) "fastest bird" AND speed
   (C) bird AND fly
   (D) speed AND fastest

Unit 4
Key Word Searching

4. How long does it take an ostrich egg to hatch?
   (A) egg AND hatch
   (B) time AND ostrich
   (C) "ostrich egg" AND hatch
   (D) hatch AND time

---

5. How hot is it inside a volcano?
   (A) volcano AND inside AND temperature
   (B) "fiery volcano"
   (C) "temperature on inside"
   (D) volcano

---

6. Who won the Stanley Cup in 1997?
   (A) Stanley AND Cup
   (B) "Stanley Cup" AND winner AND 1997
   (C) Stanley AND won
   (D) Cup AND winner

---

7. What does the Olympic symbol stand for?
   (A) Olympic symbol
   (B) symbols
   (C) Olympics AND games
   (D) "stand for" AND Olympics

---

8. How can I tell the difference between a rabbit and a hare?
   (A) "rabbit hare"
   (B) rabbit AND different
   (C) rabbit AND hare
   (D) rabbit AND hare AND difference

---

9. How do I grow a Venus flytrap?
   (A) flytrap AND Venus
   (B) grow AND "Venus flytrap"
   (C) grow AND trap
   (D) growing plants

---

10. What is the title of the first book Allen Say published?
   (A) Allen Say AND author
   (B) authors AND "first books published"
   (C) Allen Say AND "first book"
   (D) Allen Say

Unit 5
Evaluating a Web Site

Before using a Web site, it is important to decide whether the information on the site is true and complete. Some questions to ask when evaluating a Web site include the following:

- **Who is the author?** The author of a Web site should be given on the page. The author can be a person or an organization. If you do not have enough information about the author, you should not trust the information given because it might be biased or inaccurate.
- **Why was it written?** Does the site give only factual information, or is the author stating his or her opinion? If a product is being sold on the site, the information presented may be biased because the author wants you to think his or her products are the best.
- **When was it written?** A Web site should have up-to-date information. Even a new site might contain outdated information, so be sure to cross-check your research with another source, such as a current magazine article.
- **Does it have the information you need?** A site about the Special Olympics will not help you if you need information about the original Olympic Games.

Is each Web site a reliable source?

1. a Web site about the 1969 moon landing written by NASA
   (A) Yes **(B)** No

2. a Web site about the most popular new toys of the season last updated in December 1996
   (A) Yes **(B)** No

3. a Web site about the nutritional value of vitamins on a site that sells vitamins
   (A) Yes **(B)** No

4. a Web site about Colonial America written by a history professor
   (A) Yes **(B)** No

5. a Web site about how to make a volcano for a science fair, written by a science teacher
   (A) Yes **(B)** No

6. a Web site about travel in Japan written by the Japanese Board of Tourism, which is sponsored by the Japanese government
   (A) Yes **(B)** No

Unit 5

Evaluating a Web Site

7. a Web site about global warming written by the Environmental Protection Agency
   (A) Yes **(B)** No

8. a Web site about the history of the Internet with no author or sponsor listed
   (A) Yes **(B)** No

9. a Web site about how coins are made written by the United States Mint
   (A) Yes **(B)** No

10. a Web site about the life cycle of the praying mantis written by an entomologist, a person who studies insects
    (A) Yes **(B)** No

11. a Web site with official information about the United States Senate written by the United States Government
    (A) Yes **(B)** No

12. a Web site about Martin Luther King Jr. sponsored by the National Civil Rights Museum
    (A) Yes **(B)** No

13. a Web site about the sports legend Michael Jordan written by a sixth grader
    (A) Yes **(B)** No

14. a Web site about first aid procedures written by the American Red Cross
    (A) Yes **(B)** No

15. a Web site about animal welfare maintained by a nonprofit animal rescue group
    (A) Yes **(B)** No

Unit 6
Reading Graphs and Charts

Graphs and charts are drawings that give information in a way that is easy to read.

- A **pie chart** shows how a whole can be divided into parts. The main title of the chart is at the top. The specific information this type of chart gives is listed next to *or* within each section of the chart.

Computers Sold at Connected Earth Computer Store

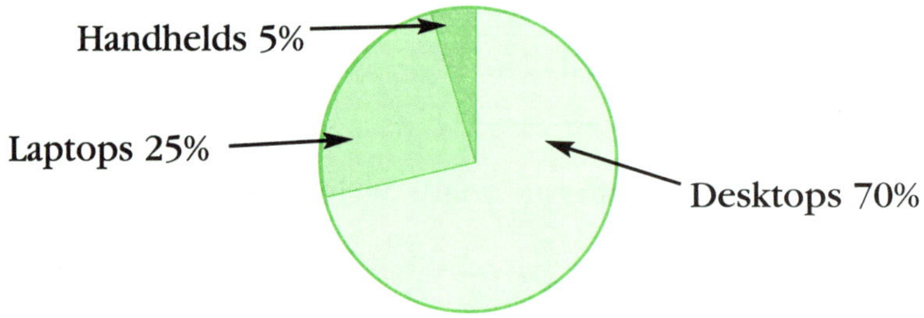

Use the pie chart below to answer each question.

Yao's Weekly Budget

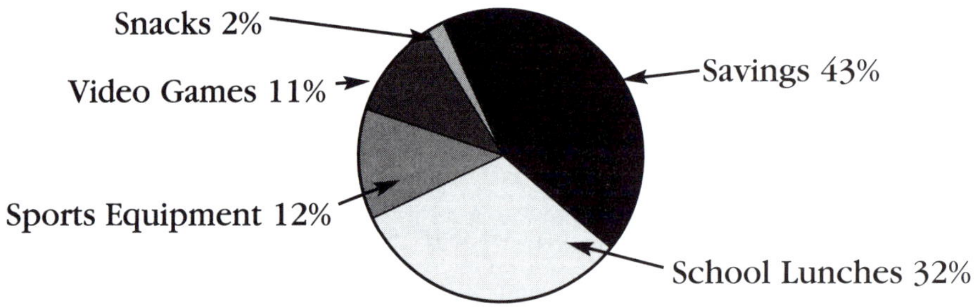

1. What percentage of Yao's weekly budget does he spend on his school lunches?
   (A) 2%
   (B) 43%
   (C) 11%
   (D) 32%

2. On what two things combined does Yao spend 23% of his budget?
   (A) Snacks and Video Games
   (B) Video Games and Sports Equipment
   (C) Sports Equipment and Snacks
   (D) Snacks and School Lunches

3. On which thing does Yao spend almost half of his budget each week?
   (A) Video Games
   (B) Snacks
   (C) Savings
   (D) Sports Equipment

Unit 6
Reading Graphs and Charts

Use the pie chart below to answer each question.

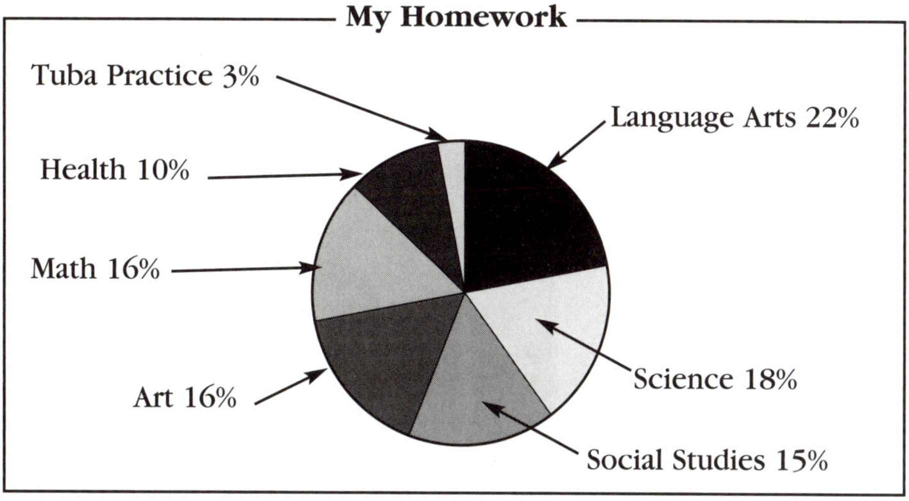

4. On which activity does Vida spend the most amount of time each week?

(A) Language Arts **(C)** Science
(B) Social Studies **(D)** Health

---

5. On which activity does Vida spend the least amount of time each week?

(A) Art **(C)** Tuba Practice
(B) Language Arts **(D)** Math

---

6. On which two activities does Vida spend the same amount of time?

(A) Language Arts and Science **(C)** Social Studies and Art
(B) Math and Art **(D)** None of the above

---

7. Which two activities combined take 25% of Vida's total homework time to complete?

(A) Math and Art **(C)** Tuba Practice and Language Arts
(B) Tuba Practice and Math **(D)** Social Studies and Science

---

8. What percentage of homework time does Vida spend on Social Studies and Science combined?

(A) 15% **(C)** 25%
(B) 18% **(D)** 33%

Unit 6
Reading Graphs and Charts

- A **bar graph** uses numbers, lines, and bars to compare information. To read a bar graph, read the title to find out what the graph is about. The information across the bottom of the graph shows the things being compared. The information on the left side of the graphs shows amounts.

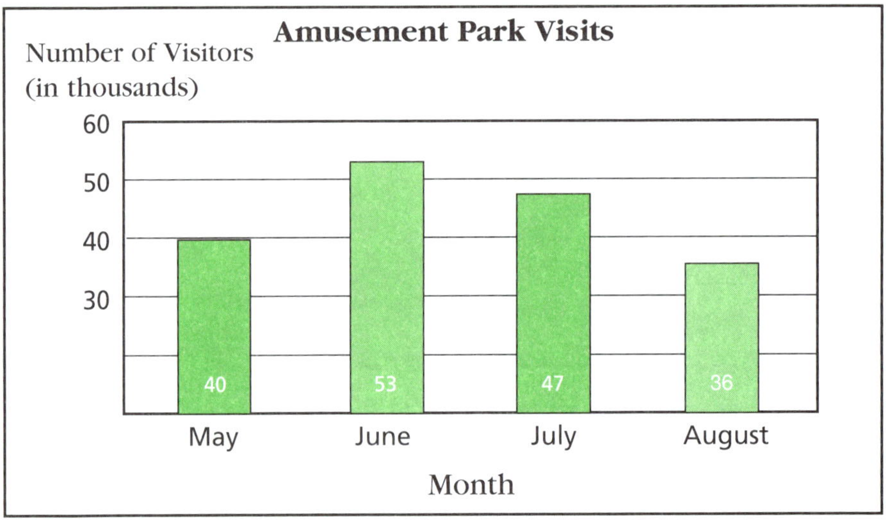

Use the bar graph below to answer the questions on the following page.

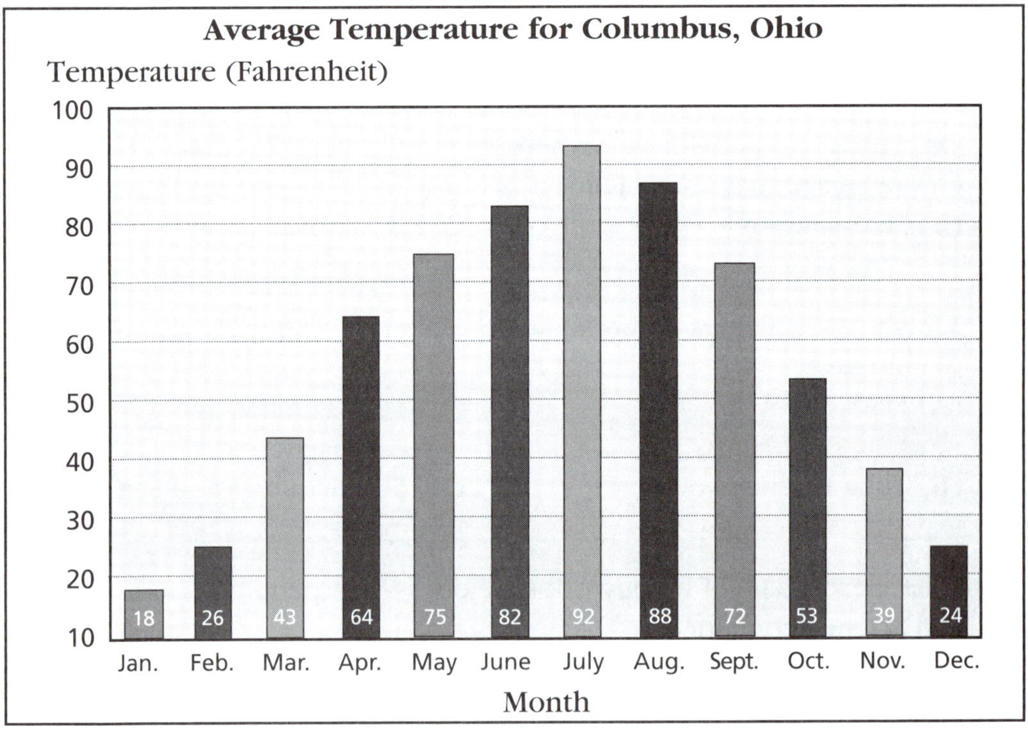

9. In which month does Columbus have the lowest average temperature?
   (A) December
   (B) February
   (C) August
   (D) January

10. In which month is Columbus the warmest?
   (A) June
   (B) July
   (C) August
   (D) September

11. Which two months' average temperatures combined are equal to July's average temperature?
   (A) February and April
   (B) October and November
   (C) January and May
   (D) September and December

12. What is the difference in average temperature between the months of January and August?
   (A) 35 degrees
   (B) 74 degrees
   (C) 70 degrees
   (D) 18 degrees

13. Which two months have average temperatures that are the closest?
   (A) July and August
   (B) August and September
   (C) May and June
   (D) January and February

14. Have many months of the year have average temperatures below 50 degrees?
   (A) four
   (B) five
   (C) two
   (D) six

15. Between which two months does the temperature change the greatest?
   (A) September and October
   (B) February and March
   (C) March and April
   (D) October and November

16. What is the difference in average temperature between the months of February and June?
   (A) 56 degrees
   (B) 70 degrees
   (C) 46 degrees
   (D) 27 degrees

The Second LAP
Language Activity Pages

A. Exercising Your Skill

You have been learning about key word searching, evaluating Web sites, and reading pie charts and bar graphs. Number your paper from 1 to 3. Choose the word or words that correctly complete each sentence.

1. A _____ shows how a whole is divided into parts.
   (A) bar graph
   (B) pie chart
   (C) key-word search
2. Use _____ around the subject you key in the search box to make your search even more specific.
   (A) commas
   (B) parentheses
   (C) quotation marks
3. A Web site with _____ information may not be reliable, so you should cross-check your research with another source.
   (A) outdated
   (B) up-to-date
   (C) complete

B. Expanding Your Skill

Number your paper from 1 to 4. Decide whether or not each Web site is a reliable source.

1. a Web site about iguanas written by Eric, a fourth-grade student who has a pet iguana
   (A) Yes **(B)** No
2. a Web site about the Roman god Vulcan with no author listed
   (A) Yes **(B)** No
3. a Web site about prairie dogs written by a reporter for a well-known science magazine
   (A) Yes **(B)** No
4. a Web site about how to treat a cold written by a doctor
   (A) Yes **(B)** No

C. Exploring Language

Expository Writing Read the paragraph. Then choose the best key words to find Web sites containing information about each question.

People share the planet with trees, flowers, insects, fish, whales, dogs, and many other plants and animals. Each species of plant or animal has its place on Earth, and each one is dependent on others. Plants give off oxygen that animals need to breathe. Animals pollinate plants and spread their seeds. Animals eat plants and are in turn eaten by larger animals. When plants and animals die, they become part of the soil in which new plants take root and grow.

1. What types of animals pollinate apple trees?
   (A) apples AND tree
   (B) apples AND pollination
   (C) animals AND pollination

2. How do plants make oxygen for animals to breathe?
   (A) plants AND oxygen
   (B) plants AND animals
   (C) oxygen AND animals

D. Expressing Yourself

Choose one of these activities. When you are finished, give your paper to your teacher.

1. Choose a topic to research, and use an Internet search engine to find information about your topic. Select key words to use in your search. Then visit at least ten Web sites from your search and evaluate each one. Make a chart like the one shown below, and fill in the information for each Web site.

Title of Web Site	Author	Sponsor	Date Written/ Updated	Date Accessed	URL	Comments

2. **WORK with a PARTNER** Do some research to find the average temperatures in your city for each month of the year. Create a bar graph to present your findings to the class.

Unit 7

Getting Ideas and Narrowing Your Topic

The first step in the research process is to **get an idea.** You might be assigned a research topic, or you might need to come up with one on your own. Ideas for topics can come from almost anywhere—questions you have, things that interest you, activities you enjoy.

- A good research topic is one that requires you to learn something new and draw your own conclusions instead of just list facts.
- A good research topic is also not too broad, or general. Your topic should be narrow, or specific, enough to write about in one research report, but not so narrow that you will not have enough ideas to write about.

Broad (General) Topic: Ocean Animals

Narrow (Specific) Topic: The Humpback Whale

Topic That Is Too Narrow: What the Humpback Whale Eats

Answer each question by imagining that you are writing a report about each topic given.

1. Which is the best way to narrow the topic *Sports* for a report?
   (A) The Game of Soccer
   (B) Popular Sports
   (C) Great Sport Players
   (D) The History of Sports

2. Which is *not* the best way to narrow the topic *Oceans* for a report?
   (A) The Atlantic Ocean
   (B) Ocean Pollution and Why It Should Be Stopped
   (C) Strange Creatures of the Pacific Ocean
   (D) Large Bodies of Water

3. Which is *not* the best way to narrow the topic *America's History* for a report?
   (A) The Story of the United States of America
   (B) The Revolutionary War
   (C) The Settling of the Colonies in Early America
   (D) 2000 Presidential Election

4. Which is *not* the best way to narrow the topic *Famous Inventions* for a report?

(A) Henry Ford and His Model T
(B) American Inventions
(C) Now That's a Bright Idea!: The First Lightbulb
(D) The Telephone and How It Works

---

5. Which is *not* the best way to narrow the topic *Transportation* for a report?
(A) How a Helicopter Flies
(B) Ocean Liners
(C) Transportation throughout the World
(D) How Do Steam Passenger Trains Work?

---

6. Which is the best way to narrow the topic *The Planets* for a report?
(A) Planets and Stars
(B) Pluto, the Smallest Planet
(C) Big Planets
(D) Space

---

7. Which is *not* the best way to narrow the topic *Computers* for a report?
(A) Computers and People
(B) Personal Computer Use in Japanese Homes
(C) How Does a CD-ROM Drive Work?
(D) Chips, Bits, and Bytes: A Brief History of the Computer

---

8. Which is *not* the best way to narrow the topic *The Human Body* for a report?
(A) The Super Circulatory System
(B) How Broken Bones Heal
(C) What Is an Appendix for Anyway?
(D) Facts about the Human Body

Unit 8
Formulating Questions

After you have narrowed your topic, think about what you want to learn about the topic you chose. Ask questions related to your topic that you want to know the answers to.

- What might you want to know about the topic *Tornadoes?*

  How does a tornado form?

  What does everyone need to know about tornado safety?

  What are the most damaging tornadoes in history?

  How many tornadoes occur in the United States each year?

- Each question you research should be related to your topic. If your topic is *Tornadoes,* you would *not* ask the question, *Where do the most hurricanes occur?*

Choose the question that is *not* specifically related to each topic.

1. Zoos

   (A) Who started the first circus?
   (B) How are animals transported to and from zoos?
   (C) What are some of the rarest animals found at zoos in the United States?
   (D) What are some of the largest zoos in the world?

2. Music

   (A) How does a clarinet make sound?
   (B) What instruments make an orchestra?
   (C) How many hours a day do dancers train?
   (D) How is music recorded on a CD?

3. Baseball

   (A) Why is baseball known as America's pastime?
   (B) What are the popular sports in other countries?
   (C) How many professional baseball teams are there?
   (D) What are the rules of baseball?

4. Airplanes

   (A) What is the fastest flying bird?
   (B) How safe is it to travel by airplane?
   (C) What is the largest airplane ever built?
   (D) What makes an airplane fly?

5. Rocks and Land Formations
   (A) How does a canyon form?
   (B) What are the differences among igneous, metamorphic, and sedimentary rocks?
   (C) How was Mammoth Cave formed?
   (D) What kinds of animals run the fastest?

---

6. Pollution
   (A) What are the types of pollution?
   (B) What types of plants grow in the city?
   (C) What damage does pollution do to plants and animals?
   (D) Is automobile exhaust bad for the environment?

---

7. The California Gold Rush
   (A) What tools did miners use to search for gold?
   (B) What started the Gold Rush?
   (C) What obstacles did the miners face?
   (D) Why don't we use gold for currency now?

---

8. Telescopes
   (A) How can we view the planets?
   (B) What is the difference between a refractor and a reflector telescope?
   (C) Can I see Jupiter with my telescope?
   (D) How does a microscope work?

---

9. Mountain Climbing
   (A) What is the tallest mountain in the United States?
   (B) What special gear do mountain climbers need?
   (C) Is climbing a mountain safe?
   (D) Why do mountain climbers need additional oxygen?

---

10. Dogs
   (A) Do dogs need a lot of exercise?
   (B) What is the most popular dog breed in the United States?
   (C) Why do wolves howl?
   (D) How do you train a dog?

Unit 9

Making a Research Statement

Once you have thought of questions to ask about your topic, you can write a **research statement,** or thesis statement, based on your questions. Then your research can prove or disprove your statement.

Research Statement	**Question**
America's most effective president was Abraham Lincoln.	Who has been America's most effective president?

Which question is the basis for each research statement?

1. English is becoming the world language.
   (A) How many people speak English?
   (B) What languages are spoken in Europe?
   (C) Is there a language that everyone in the world can understand?

2. More people speak Chinese than any other language.
   (A) Which language is spoken by the most people?
   (B) How many different kinds of languages are there?
   (C) Where is Chinese spoken?

3. Spanish is spoken in many different countries around the world.
   (A) Is Spanish an easy language to learn?
   (B) Should Spanish be taught in all schools in America?
   (C) Where is Spanish spoken?

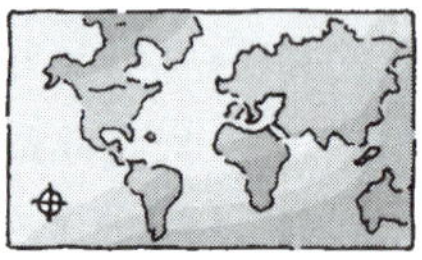

4. Hindi is the language spoken by the second most number of people, but mainly by people only in India.
   (A) Is Hindi the only language spoken in India?
   (B) How many people speak Hindi?
   (C) Why couldn't Hindi be the world language?

5. Spanish is spoken by more people than French because of the Spanish explorers.
   (A) Why do more people speak Spanish than French?
   (B) Is it better to take Spanish or French in high school?
   (C) Where is French spoken?

Unit 9

Making a Research Statement

6. Because of the Internet, English should be the world language.
   (A) How many people speak English?
   (B) Why isn't English the most spoken language in the world?
   (C) Is English a good choice for a world language?

---

7. Many languages are spoken in the United States because of immigration.
   (A) How many languages are spoken in the United States?
   (B) Why are so many languages spoken in the United States?
   (C) Should English be the only national language in the United States?

---

8. Spanish is the second most spoken language in the United States after English because of immigration.
   (A) Should the United States have two national languages?
   (B) Should everyone be required to take Spanish in high school?
   (C) Why do so many people speak Spanish in the United States?

---

9. Studying Latin can actually help you improve your English.
   (A) Was Latin spoken in many countries?
   (B) Why is Latin no longer spoken?
   (C) Why should anyone learn Latin today?

---

10. Chinese and Hindi are not good choices for a world language because they are not spoken in many different countries.
    (A) Should everyone learn Chinese and Hindi?
    (B) How many people speak Chinese and Hindi?
    (C) Why shouldn't Chinese or Hindi become the world's language?

---

11. Everyone should learn to speak at least two languages.
    (A) What are the most popular languages?
    (B) How can people learn to communicate with people from other countries?
    (C) How many different languages are there?

---

12. Learning a second language should begin in elementary school.
    (A) How many students take Spanish in school?
    (B) When is the best time to learn a second language?
    (C) What are the benefits of learning a second language?

Unit 10
Identifying Sources

Once you have your research statement, you need to gather information to prove or disprove your statement. There are many different sources of information in addition to books. Most of the sources below can be found on the Internet or at a library.

- An **almanac** includes lists, statistics, facts, and figures. You would use an almanac to find the most spoken languages in the United States.
- An **atlas** is a book of maps. You would use an atlas to find the name of the county in which Miami, Florida, is located.
- An **encyclopedia** includes general information about many topics. Encyclopedia entries may be one paragraph to several pages long. Encyclopedia entries do *not* include information about current events.
- An **expert** is someone who is especially knowledgeable about a topic. Most experts work in a professional setting. Interviewing an expert is one way of researching a topic for a report.
- A **newspaper** mainly reports on current events. Some newspapers, such as *The New York Times*, focus on reporting news from around the nation and around the world. Smaller, local newspapers focus on reporting local news.
- A **magazine** includes feature articles on current events or other topics of interest. Feature articles are similar to newspaper articles, but they are usually longer and provide more details.

Choose the best source to use to find each type of information. If both are good sources for that kind of information, choose *Both*.

1. a map of Uganda
   (A) almanac
   (B) atlas
   (C) Both

2. general information about archaeology
   (A) newspaper
   (B) encyclopedia
   (C) Both

3. current events occurring in your city
   (A) newspaper
   (B) almanac
   (C) Both

4. the type of work that a botanist, a scientist who studies plants, does
   (A) encyclopedia
   (B) expert
   (C) Both

5. information about how to become a marine biologist
   (A) expert
   (B) newspaper
   (C) both

6. the top ten most populous states
   (A) magazine
   (B) almanac
   (C) Both

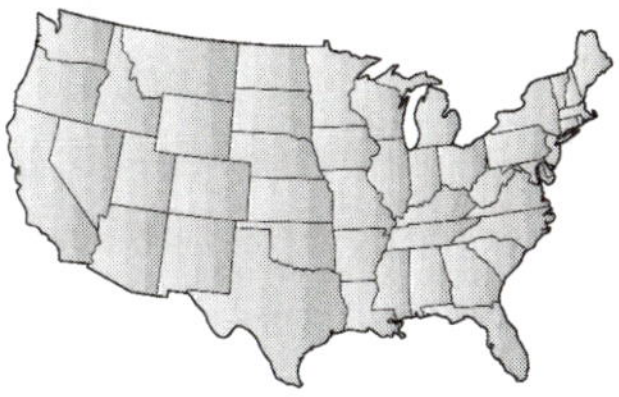

7. a list of the most profitable companies in Japan
   (A) magazine
   (B) atlas
   (C) Both

8. a day in the life of a New York firefighter
   (A) encyclopedia
   (B) expert
   (C) Both

9. information about Richard Nixon's presidency
   (A) encyclopedia
   (B) atlas
   (C) Both

10. recent births and deaths in a particular city
   (A) almanac
   (B) newspaper
   (C) Both

Unit 11

Comparing Information across Sources

You should use several different sources to find the information you need when writing a research paper. Look at many sources, and compare the information you find in each. Using a variety of sources will not only help you get more information, it will also help you get accurate information.

Read the following three sources of information about the *Titanic*, and then answer the questions.

Encyclopedia Entry

Titanic. The *Titanic* was a British luxury passenger ship made by the White Star Line. At the time it was built, the *Titanic* was the largest ship to sail the seas. It had a double-bottomed hull and sixteen compartments that were designed to be watertight. Because of these safety features, the *Titanic* was thought to be unsinkable. The builders of the *Titanic* were so certain the ship could not sink that they provided only enough lifeboats for about half the passengers on board.

During its maiden voyage in April 1912, the *Titanic* struck an iceberg broadside, ripping a 300-foot gash into the hull of the ship. When the accident happened, the passengers did not panic. They felt the mighty ship could never sink. Even when the crew began loading people onto the lifeboats, many still did not believe they were in danger. The ship sank during the early morning hours of April 15; about 1,500 lives were lost. Approximately 700 people survived the shipwreck.

In 1985 a French and American crew found the wreck of the *Titanic* on the ocean floor. It was found lying upright in two pieces at a depth of about 13,000 feet. Many trips have since been made to the wreckage to take photographs and to retrieve artifacts.

Excerpt from a Magazine Interview

I was awakened from my sleep by a knock at our stateroom door. My father arose from the desk where he was working to answer it. I saw a crewmember whisper something to my father, and then Father shut the door. Mother had also been awakened by the knock and was looking to my father for an explanation. I sat up in my bed, and Father told us that we were to get dressed and go above-board immediately. I was scared, but I saw no panic in my father's eyes. I dressed quickly and quietly and waited for Mother. When she was ready, Father took each of us by the hand and led us to the deck. There I saw scores of women and children with life preservers being helped onto lifeboats. Father waited with us until we were given a seat on one of the boats. He kissed us both and told us that he would see us soon. I glanced at my mother and saw tears filling her eyes. Father quickly strode away to help others onto the lifeboats. That was the last time I ever saw him.

As mother and I floated on the sea, I looked at the empty seats in the lifeboat and wished mightily that my father could have joined us. Suddenly, I heard a loud roar, and I watched in amazement as one of the massive funnels gave way and crashed into the ocean. People were screaming and jumping into the frigid ocean water. As we waited shivering in the small lifeboat, I saw the lights on the *Titanic* flicker and then go out before the bow of the great ship slipped below the surface of the water. Soon after, our little boat was picked up by the crew of the *Carpathia,* and we were taken to safety.

Now as an old woman I hear of the expeditions seeking the wreckage of the *Titanic*. I can understand the curiosity of a new generation about the tragedy; but my wish is that the great ship will never be found and that the people who lost their lives aboard it will stay at rest in their watery graves.

Unit 11
Comparing Information across Sources

Time Line

The Sinking of the Titanic, April 1912

April10

9:30-11:30 A.M.: Passengers arrive and board the *Titanic.*

12:00 P.M.: *Titanic* casts off and begins its maiden voyage.

April11

1:30 P.M.: The *Titanic* departs from Queenstown Harbor. The last known photograph of the intact ship is taken. The *Titanic* sails approximately 900 miles in calm seas the first three days.

April14

The *Titanic* receives at least seven ice warnings during the day.

11:40 P.M.: An iceberg is spotted straight ahead, but it is too late to avoid a collision. The iceberg scrapes along the starboard bow of the ship. Water begins pouring into the ship.

April15

12:00 A.M.: The captain of the *Titanic* is told by the ship's designer that the vessel will be able to remain afloat for only a few more hours.

12:05 A.M.: Orders are given to bring the passengers to the deck and begin loading them onto the lifeboats. There is only enough room in the lifeboats for 1,178 of the estimated 2,227 on board.

12:15 A.M.: A number of ships in the area hear *Titanic's* distress signals and prepare to assist in the rescue.

12:25 A.M.: The lifeboats begin to be loaded with women and children. Many boats are lowered without being filled to capacity.

2:05 A.M.: One of the last of the lifeboats departs from the ship.

2:17 A.M.: *Titanic's* captain releases his crew to try to save themselves; many jump overboard. *Titanic's* bow is submerged.

2:18 A.M.: The ship breaks in two, and the bow sinks into the ocean.

2:20 A.M.: The stern begins to sink slowly into the water; over 1,500 people perish in the disaster.

4:10 A.M.: The first lifeboat is picked up by a rescue ship.

8:30 A.M.: The last lifeboat is picked up.

8:50 A.M.: The rescue ship leaves the wreckage site headed toward New York with 705 survivors on board.

[end box]

Unit 11
Comparing Information across Sources

1. Which source gives an eyewitness account of the sinking of the *Titanic*?
   (A) the magazine
   (B) the encyclopedia
   (C) the time line

2. From which source do we learn that at the time the *Titanic* was built, it was the largest ship ever to sail?
   (A) the magazine
   (B) the encyclopedia
   (C) the time line

3. Which source gives the most detailed information about the disaster?
   (A) the magazine
   (B) the encyclopedia
   (C) the time line

4. From which source(s) do we learn that the lifeboats were not full when they were lowered into the ocean?
   (A) the magazine only
   (B) the time line only
   (C) the magazine and the time line

5. Which source tells about the ice warnings the *Titanic* received?
   (A) the magazine
   (B) the encyclopedia
   (C) the time line

6. Which sources reveal that the *Titanic* struck an iceberg?
   (A) the magazine and the time line
   (B) the encyclopedia and the time line
   (C) the magazine and the encyclopedia

The Third LAP
Language Activity Pages

A. Exercising Your Skill

You have been learning how to get ideas for a research report, formulate questions, develop a research statement, and find information to prove or disprove your research. You have also learned to compare information across a variety of sources. Number your paper from 1 to 3, and answer the following questions about what you have learned.

1. What is not an important factor when choosing a topic?
   (A) The topic should be narrow enough so that you can find specific information about it.
   (B) You should be able to draw your own conclusions about the topic rather than just list facts.
   (C) You already know about the topic.

2. Why is a research statement important?
   (A) It focuses on the main point of your research paper that you will prove or disprove through your research.
   (B) It explains why you chose your topic.
   (C) It summarizes all your research.

3. Why is it important to compare information across sources?
   (A) You may need more information than one source provides.
   (B) You may need to verify that your sources are accurate.
   (C) Both A and B.

B. Expanding Your Skill

Choose the best source to use to find information on each given topic.

1. the capital of South Dakota
   (A) atlas
   (B) expert
   (C) magazine

2. a list of the president's faces on United States coins
   (A) almanac
   (B) atlas
   (C) encyclopedia

C. Exploring Language

Expository Writing Read the following paragraph from a research report, and answer the questions.

> Although Chinese, Hindi, and Spanish are spoken by more people in the world, English should be the world language. English is the most popular second language in the world. It is also spoken in more countries than any other language. English is the predominant language of the Internet, which is globalizing the nations of the world.

1. What central question does the paragraph answer?
   (A) Why should English be the world language?
   (B) What are the world's most popular languages?
   (C) What is the most popular second language?

2. What is the best research statement for this research report?
   (A) English should be the world language.
   (B) The most spoken languages are Chinese and Hindi.
   (C) English is the most popular second language.

3. What would be the best source to use to find information for this report?
   (A) a nonfiction book about languages
   (B) an almanac that lists the populations of the world's countries
   (C) an atlas that includes a world map

D. Expressing Yourself

Choose one of these activities. When you are finished, give your paper to your teacher.

1. **WORK with a PARTNER** Work through the steps of the research process with a partner. First, brainstorm an idea for a research topic. Then, write at least three questions about the topic you chose. Next, write a research statement. Finally, list at least three sources of information for this topic.

2. Make a list of three topics you would be interested in researching. Then, write a research statement for each topic.

Unit 12
Taking Notes

When you are researching your topic, take notes as you read. This will help you remember important facts and details. Each note you write should answer a question you have about your topic.

What were the Spanish-conquered areas in the New World called?
–New Spain
–New Granada
–Peru
–La Plata

Read the first section of the following passage about the Iceman. Then complete each note card.

Ötzi the Iceman

Ötzi the Iceman is a 5,000-year-old mummy that was found frozen in melting glacial ice in the Alps in 1991. Ötzi lived during the Bronze Age and was probably a hunter or a shepherd. He is the oldest mummy ever discovered.

When Ötzi was first discovered by Helmut and Erika Simon, they thought the corpse was the remains of a mountain climber who had gotten lost in the Alps. The Simons took a picture of Ötzi and then returned to the hotel where they were vacationing. Along the way, they stopped to report their find. The authorities were not surprised to hear of the frozen body. Just a few weeks before, the bodies of two people who had set out to hike the mountain in 1934 were found. They thought Ötzi was just another hiker who had not returned from a climb.

Because the people who came to retrieve Ötzi did not realize he was so special, no great care was taken with his body. His rescuers used a stick that they had found close by to try to pry him free from the ice. It was later discovered that the "stick" was really Ötzi's bow. Another man tried to use a jackhammer to free him and ended up drilling a hole into Ötzi's hip. Others tried to grab onto the Iceman's clothing to yank him from the ice but ended up only tearing his garments. When Ötzi was finally freed, he was shoved into a coffin, and one of his arms was broken in the process.

Unit 12
Taking Notes

Who is Ötzi?
—oldest mummy
—lived during Bronze Age
—_____

1. Which note completes the note card?
   (A) hiker
   (B) hunter or shepherd
   (C) discovered the Iceman
   (D) mountain climber

When, where, and by whom was Ötzi discovered?
—1991
—Alps
—_____

2. Which note completes the note card?
   (A) hikers Helmut and Erika Simon
   (B) the authorities
   (C) rescuers
   (D) mountain climbers

What mistakes were made during the retrieval of Ötzi's body?
—used bow as a tool
—torn clothing
—arm was broken
—_____

3. Which note completes the note card?
   (A) took a picture
   (B) tried to free him from the ice
   (C) drilled into his hip with jackhammer
   (D) was finally freed

Unit 12
Taking Notes

Read the second section of the passage about the Iceman. Then complete each note card.

Once it was revealed how old Ötzi was, scientists were eager to study him. They knew that the Iceman's body would give them important information about how Bronze Age people lived. The scientists looked at his clothing and even made replicas of his shoes. Some were interested in the artifacts found near the body, such as arrows, a backpack, a knife, and a medicine bag. Other scientists looked at the contents of the Iceman's intestines and colon to discover the types of foods he ate. It was found that his last meals consisted of wild goat, deer, barley, and another grain called *einkorn.*

One of the Iceman's biggest secrets was how he died. Many believed he had simply grown tired and had frozen to death before he could find shelter. Some scientists thought Ötzi had broken ribs, and they theorized that he might have died from a fight or a fall that had caused the injury. In 2001 it was discovered that Ötzi had actually died from an arrowhead that had been shot into his body.

Today Ötzi is located at the South Tyrol Museum of Archaeology in Bolzano, Italy, where visitors can view his body through a small window. His body lies in an exhibit that is kept at 21.2 degrees Fahrenheit. Sensors constantly measure his weight to make certain there are no changes in his body tissues.

Unit 12
Taking Notes

What were some artifacts found near Ötzi 's body?
—arrows
—backpack
—knife
—_____

4. Which note completes the note card?
   (A) wild goat
   (B) medicine bag
   (C) spear
   (D) eating utensils

What foods did scientists discover the Iceman ate shortly before he died?
—wild goat
—deer
—barley
—_____

5. Which note completes the note card?
   (A) arrowhead
   (B) fish
   (C) rabbit
   (D) einkorn

Where is the Iceman now?
—Bolzano, Italy
—special chamber that is 21.2 degrees
—_____

6. Which note completes the note card?
   (A) enclosed in glacial ice
   (B) buried in the Alps
   (C) South Tyrol Museum of Archaeology
   (D) Egypt

Unit 13

Summarizing

A **summary** briefly reviews the main points of a reading selection. Writers use summaries of information to support their research statements.

- To write a summary, look for the most important points in the selection. Then write them in your own words. Writing about someone else's ideas in your own words is called **paraphrasing.**

Read each paragraph. Then choose the summary that best answers the question.

Seasons happen because Earth makes one full revolution around the sun each year. While making its revolution, Earth is tipped on its axis. In June, Earth's northern hemisphere is tipped toward the sun, and its southern hemisphere is tipped away. In December, the reverse of this is true.

1. Why do seasons happen?
   (A) Seasons happen because of Earth's tilt on its axis as it revolves around the sun.
   (B) Seasons happen because the northern hemisphere is tipped toward the sun.
   (C) Seasons happen because Earth is tipped away from the sun in December.

In the spring, frogs begin a new life cycle. A female frog will lay her eggs in warm, shallow water so they can incubate. When the eggs hatch, tadpoles emerge. They survive by eating tiny plants they find in the water. The nourishment from the plants helps the tadpoles grow bigger and develop lungs and legs. Finally, tadpoles' tails are absorbed into their bodies, and they become adult frogs.

2. What is the life cycle of a frog?
   (A) Tadpoles are born and then become frogs after a while.
   (B) Frogs lay their eggs in warm water, and then the tadpoles eat tiny plants to survive.
   (C) Tadpoles hatch from eggs, spend time in the water maturing, and then become frogs.

Unit 13
Summarizing

Plants have various ways of adapting to winter weather. Small plants, such as daisies and other flowers, survive harsh winters because of their deep root systems that are below the reach of frost. Evergreen trees have leaves that are thin and shiny, which makes it hard for snow to stick to them. Trees such as maples and oaks lose their leaves before winter in an effort to save their resources. This helps their roots survive so they can regrow leaves in the spring.

3. How do plants survive in winter?
   (A) Small plants and some trees are able to survive harsh winters because of their root systems, while other trees survive because their leaves repel snow.
   (B) Evergreens have thin, glossy leaves, and snow cannot stick to them.
   (C) Snow can't get to the roots of plants like daisies.

Snowfall accumulations can be difficult to measure. Many times snow melts when it lands on the ground because of warm soil, wind, or sunshine. It is also very easily blown around into drifts while leaving other areas almost barren. Depending on how dense it is, snow can settle either very quickly or very slowly.

4. Why is it sometimes difficult to measure snow?
   (A) Snow melts when it lands and leaves barren areas.
   (B) Snow can be dense and be blown around.
   (C) Snow can melt, be blown away, or settle irregularly.

There are many holidays celebrated during the winter season. In the Northern Hemisphere, the most popular winter festival is Christmas. Another holiday is the Jewish festival Chanukah, which lasts eight days. The Chinese New Year is also celebrated in the winter. It features fireworks and parades of actors dressed up as dragons.

5. What are some of the popular winter holidays?
   (A) Chanukah, a Jewish winter holiday, is eight days long.
   (B) Christmas, Chanukah, and the Chinese New Year are popular winter holidays.
   (C) The Chinese New Year is celebrated with fireworks.

Unit 14
Writing an Outline

When writing a report or research paper, it is helpful to create an **outline.** An outline provides a loose guideline for the report. It helps writers keep their ideas organized. An outline includes topics, subtopics, and details under each subtopic.

Use the outline below to answer the questions on the following page.

TOPIC
I. What to Plant in a Garden

SUBTOPIC
A. Vegetables
  1. Carrots
  2. U
  3. Okra
  4. Squash

SUBTOPIC
B. Fruits
  1. Melon
    a. Watermelon
    b. V
  2. W
    a. X
    b. Blueberries

SUBTOPIC
C. Flowers
  1. Bushes
    a. Roses
    b. Y Butterfly Bushes
  2. Bulbs
    a. Tulips
    b. Irises
  3. Z
    a. Daisies
    b. Petunias
    c. Poppies

Unit 14
Writing an Outline

Writing an Outline

1. Which of these belongs in the space marked U?
   (A) Fertilizer
   (B) Lilies
   (C) Water
   (D) Cucumbers

2. Which of these belongs in the space marked V?
   (A) Cantaloupe
   (B) Blueberries
   (C) Lilies
   (D) Sunflowers

3. Which of these belongs in the space marked W?
   (A) Fruit
   (B) Berries
   (C) Herbs
   (D) Potatoes

4. Which of these belongs in the space marked X?
   (A) Corn
   (B) Peas
   (C) Strawberries
   (D) Sweet Potatoes

5. Which of these belongs in the space marked Y?
   (A) Sunlight
   (B) Butterfly Bushes
   (C) Flowers
   (D) Dandelions

6. Which of these belongs in the space marked Z?
   (A) Seeds
   (B) Weeds
   (C) Grass
   (D) Bell Peppers

Unit 15
Writing Introductory Paragraphs

Once you have done your research and written an outline of your ideas to prove or disprove your research statement, you are ready to start writing. As you write, you may find you need to do more research to support your case.

- A simple way to organize your research paper is in five paragraphs. The **introductory paragraph** includes your research, or thesis, statement. The next three paragraphs are **supporting paragraphs** and present your arguments. The **concluding paragraph** summarizes your arguments and restates your research statement.
- The introductory paragraph is important because it explains what your research is about and why it matters. A good way to organize an introductory paragraph is like a funnel.

Broad statement that tells the importance of your topic
The arguments against your topic
Research statement

Choose the best thesis statement for each introductory paragraph.

1. Communication in today's information age is vitally important. Effective communication makes trading between nations easier and aids in solving global problems. The question is, which language should be the world language? Some may think that the world language should be Chinese, the one spoken by the most people.

(A) English, however, is the best choice for global communications.
(B) Over one billion people live in China.
(C) People around the world enjoy eating Chinese food

---

2. Obesity among children has become a major health issue. Some people think children will form proper eating habits if they are left to make choices about food on their own, but that is not true.

(A) Children watch too much television.
(B) Families and schools are both responsible for making sure children maintain healthful weights.
(C) Children today don't get enough exercise.

3. Fast food is everywhere. From street vendors to food courts, fast food has become a major part of the modern diet and a main source of nourishment for millions of people. Some people believe that all fast food is laden with calories and poor nutrition.

(A) Interestingly, hamburgers and French fries are eaten by millions of people every day.

(B) However, people can make healthy choices at fast-food restaurants.

(C) There are Chinese and Mexican fast food restaurants.

---

4. The United States National Parks are national treasures. Thousands of people visit our national parks each year. Some people approve of allowing private companies to use the national parks' land for things such as oil drilling, logging, cattle grazing, or snowmobiling.

(A) Instead of being slowly destroyed, our national parks should be preserved as they are for future generations to enjoy.

(B) Yellowstone, Carlsbad Caverns, and Gettysburg are just a few of our national parks.

(C) Natural gas and coal may be found in some national parks.

---

5. Founded in 1800, the Library of Congress is the largest library in the world. It has over 126 million items and about 530 miles of shelves. Sadly, some take this great resource for granted.

(A) There are 460 languages represented in the Library of Congress.

(B) The largest book in the Library of Congress is *Birds of America,* which contains John James Audubon's life-size illustrations.

(C) We should all realize that the Library of Congress is an invaluable storehouse of human memory that must be protected.

---

6. The 1998 baseball season was the most thrilling one in years. Mark McGuire and Sammy Sosa both broke Roger Maris's home-run record, while the Yankees set a major league record of wins. In the United States, surveys often show that football is the most popular sport.

(A) Even if that is true, baseball is definitely the most exciting major league sport.

(B) Cal Ripken Jr. ended his playing streak when he sat out a game.

(C) New York beat the San Diego Padres in four straight games.

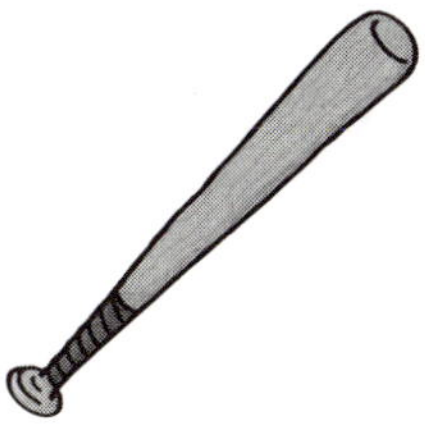

Unit 15
Writing Introductory Paragraphs

Choose the best thesis statement for each introductory paragraph.

7. Little League Baseball is the largest youth sports program in the world. It began in 1939 in Williamsport, Pennsylvania, with thirty boys playing on three teams. Some people feel that children shouldn't participate in competitive sports.

(A) Today over three million boys and girls play on 200,000 Little League teams.
(B) Those critics should realize that Little League Baseball is a great experience for boys and girls alike.
(C) Over ninety countries have Little League Baseball teams.

---

8. Dr. James Naismith invented basketball in 1891 in Springfield, Massachusetts. At first, each team had nine players instead of five. Although soccer and baseball have been very popular among children, basketball is the most popular.

(A) Basketball is fast becoming America's favorite sport.
(B) Dr. Naismith used peach baskets instead of hoops.
(C) The National Basketball Association (NBA) was formed in 1949.

---

9. The NCAA, National Collegiate Athletic Association for college basketball, began in 1939. Today it has sixty-four teams. Although other sports get a lot of attention, the Final Four weekend, when the semi-finals and finals are played, is one of the most watched sports events in the United States.

(A) Soon there may be more than sixty-four teams in the NCAA.
(B) College basketball has become a huge sport.
(C) The NCAA Tournament for women's basketball began in 1982.

---

10. Starting in 1994, the winter and summer Olympic Games have been held two years apart instead of the same year. Winter sports include bobsled, ice hockey, figure skating, and snowboarding. Summer games include baseball, canoeing, swimming, gymnastics, and track and field. Although some prefer professional or college sports, the Olympic Games are followed around the world.

(A) The Winter Olympics were first held in 1924.
(B) Both the Winter and Summer Olympics showcase the world's finest athletes.
(C) In 1900, women competed in the Olympic Games for the first time.

11. Chess is a game of skill for two players. The point is to trap the opponent's king. Chess was invented almost two thousand years ago in India. Today there are highly competitive national chess tournaments. Although many people prefer sports, chess does have its audience.

(A) The word *chess* comes from the Persian word *shah,* which means "king."

(B) Chess can be as competitive as football, basketball, or baseball.

(C) Chess is played on a chessboard divided into sixty-four squares.

---

12. Board games like chess, checkers, and backgammon are played all over the world. Board games involve strategy and skill. Winning is often a combination of skill and luck. Although winning isn't always possible, young children who play board games tend to do better in school.

(A) Board games are fun, but they also sharpen mental skills.

(B) Many board games were played in ancient times.

(C) There are many computer versions of popular board games.

---

13. Golf began in Scotland in the 1400s. The first golf course in the United States opened in 1888. Although many people prefer other sports, millions of people of all ages play golf for fun.

(A) Golf is a great sport that can be played well into old age.

(B) Learning to swing a golf club properly can be challenging.

(C) The four major championships on the men's tour are the British Open, U.S. Open, PGA Championship, and the Masters Tournament.

---

14. The first Olympic Games were played in Greece more than 2,500 years ago. They began in 776 B.C. with just a foot race. Later, boxing, wrestling, chariot racing, and the pentathlon, which includes five different events, were added. Some people forget that ancient cultures have influenced our lives today.

(A) The ancient Olympic Games were held every four years.

(B) The first modern Olympic Games were held in 1896 in Athens, Greece.

(C) The Olympic Games are a prime example of the influence ancient Greek civilization had on the world.

Unit 16

Writing Supporting Paragraphs

Once you have written your introductory paragraph and stated your thesis, the next paragraphs in your research paper should support your thesis. You should try to have at least three supporting paragraphs.

- Each **supporting paragraph** should have a topic sentence and evidence that supports the topic sentence. Try to have at least three pieces of evidence to support each topic sentence. Your evidence will come from the research you have done. As you write, you may find you need to do more research to find more evidence to support your statements. The statements that include evidence are underlined in the supporting paragraph below.

The jobs of tomorrow will be in the information and service industries. One of the fastest growing occupations is in computer science. Health and medical fields are also growing. Human services, such as social work and child care, are also on the rise. Students of today would be wise to investigate these fields.

Choose the best supporting statement for each topic sentence.

1. Americans care more about recreation than they do about education.
   (A) Americans spend over $450 billion on recreation each year, but only $130 billion on educational expenses.
   (B) Recreation includes books, magazines, toys, and videos.
   (C) Americans also spend more money on food and tobacco than on education.

2. Medical costs are skyrocketing out of control.
   (A) Medical costs include medical and dental care.
   (B) Americans spend over $950 billion on medical and dental care annually, more than on food or housing.
   (C) It takes years of education to become a doctor.

3. By analyzing spending patterns, you can tell which things impact the average American's budget the most.
   (A) Americans spend the most on medical care, food, and housing, because those are basic needs.
   (B) Every American should keep a budget.
   (C) People also need clothing.

4. Another large part of each American's budget is transportation.
   (A) Transportation includes cards, gasoline, and tickets for trains, buses, and planes.
   (B) In the future, more cars may run on electricity than on fuel.
   (C) After medical, food, and housing expenses, Americans spend the most on transportation.

5. Recreation has become a basic necessity in today's America, but it is also costly.
   (A) Americans spend over $450 billion a year on recreation, almost as much as on household expenses.
   (B) After a hard day at school or work, people need to relax.
   (C) People do a variety of things in their spare time, including reading and watching television, which cost very little money.

6. Women made major inroads into the workforce in the last half of the twentieth century.
   (A) Today there are more women in managerial and professional positions than in the past.
   (B) There are still more men than women in repair and craft jobs.
   (C) There are still more men than women in farming, forestry, and fishing.

7. Apart from managerial positions, women's jobs are mainly in administrative and service occupations.
   (A) There are over twenty-five million women and only fourteen million men in administrative jobs, which include salespeople, technicians, and clerical workers.
   (B) Many men are machine operators, laborers, and assemblers.
   (C) Human services is a growing field for men and women.

8. There are many more men than women in farming, forestry, and fishing jobs.
   (A) There are fewer farming jobs than there used to be.
   (B) Farming has changed from many small family farms to few large corporate farms.
   (C) There are almost three million men but only a half million women in farming, forestry, and fishing jobs.

Unit 17
Writing Concluding Paragraphs

A concluding paragraph summarizes your research and restates your thesis. The concluding paragraph should explain how you proved your thesis and why it is important.

- A good organization for a concluding paragraph is an inverted funnel.

Restate
your thesis.
Summarize the research.
Write a broad statement
that tells the importance of your topic.

Read the example of a concluding paragraph below.

The ways in which Americans spend their money is an effective indicator of American priorities. Necessities such as medical and dental care, food, housing, and transportation are the top priorities. Charitable contributions and educational expenses are lesser priorities. If people want more money for schools, they have to find a way to make the basic necessities more affordable.

Choose the best concluding paragraph for each underlined thesis statement.

1. **(A)** Vitamins are vital. Taking vitamins translates into higher IQ's, fewer infections, less heart disease, and less cancer. There are enormous health benefits for taking one multivitamin each day.
   (B) Vitamins are vital. Many people don't eat well. Exercising each day can help them stay healthy. Bodies and brains function better when people are physically fit and active.

2. **(A)** There is no correlation between the size of a state and the population of that state. The largest state, Alaska, has fewer people than the smallest state, Rhode Island. The United States government needs to reconsider the amount of power that each state has based on population rather than size.
   (B) There is no correlation between the size of a state and the population of that state. Alaska has just over a half million people. Rhode Island has almost one million people. Texas is second in population and size. California is first in population and third in size. New York is third in population and twenty-seventh in size.

Unit 17

Writing Concluding Paragraphs

3. **(A)** Utah is a state with many wonders. Five of the fifty-four national parks are located in Utah, each with its own distinct landforms. Utah is worth a visit.

(B) Utah is a state with many wonders. Its national parks are Arches, Bryce Canyon, Canyonlands, Capitol Reef, and Zion. Zion was established in 1919. It has Indian cliff dwellings over 1,000 years old.

4. **(A)** Alaska, the Last Frontier, has eight national parks of the fifty-four national narks for good reason. These include Denali, Gates of the Arctic, Glacier Bay, Katmai, Kenai Fjords, Kobuk Valley, Lake Clark, and Wrangell-Saint Elias.

(B) Alaska, the Last Frontier, has eight national parks of the fifty-four national narks for good reason. It is the largest state, but it also has the most spectacular scenery. Protecting the parks and preserving the Alaskan wilderness should be a national priority.

5. **(A)** Washington state is incredibly varied. The eastern part of the state is a flat desert. The western part of the state is a rain forest. It also is the home of volcanoes and beautiful mountain ranges. Washington is a fascinating place to visit and live.

(B) Washington state is incredibly varied. It has three of the fifty-four national parks. These include Mount Rainier, North Cascades, and Olympic. Volcanoes, mountains, and rain forests are in these parks.

6. **(A)** California is a great vacation spot. Not only does it have large, interesting cities, it has eight of the fifty-four national parks. A visit to California will provide a wealth of interesting things to see and do.

(B) California is a great vacation spot. Its largest cities are Los Angeles, San Diego, San Jose, and San Francisco. Its national parks are Channel Islands, Death Valley, Joshua Tree, Kings Canyon, Lassen Volcanic, Redwood, Sequoia, and Yosemite.

Unit 17

Writing Concluding Paragraphs

Choose the best concluding paragraph for each underlined thesis statement.

7. **(A)** Little League is a great experience for boys and girls alike. Little League Baseball is the largest youth sports program in the world. It began in 1939 in Williamsport Pennsylvania with thirty boys playing on three teams.

   (B) Little League is a great experience for boys and girls alike. Over three million boys and girls play on 200,000 Little League teams. It gives them physical activity and a chance to learn how to play with others. These are things that will benefit them all their lives.

---

8. **(A)** Basketball is fast becoming America's favorite sport. Dr. James Naismith invented basketball in 1891 in Springfield, Massachusetts. He used peach baskets instead of hoops.

   (B) Basketball is fast becoming America's favorite sport. It is the most popular sport among children. Between college basketball's Final Four and the NBA, hundreds of thousands of people follow the sport. Basketball is fun to play and to watch.

---

9. **(A)** Football could be America's most popular sport. College football and its Bowl Championships and professional football are among the most watched sports events in America.

   (B) Football could be America's most popular sport. Walter Camp is credited with determining there would be eleven players on each football team. Walter Camp introduced "downs" and was the first to have the field lined with chalk every five yards.

---

10. **(A)** Chess can be as competitive as football, basketball, or baseball. The word *chess* comes from the Persian word *shah* which means "king." Chess is a game of skill for two players. The point is to trap the opponent's king.

    (B) Chess can be as competitive as football, basketball, or baseball. There are highly competitive national chess tournaments and computer chess games. Many people find the same thrill in chess that others find in competitive sports.

Unit 17
Writing Concluding Paragraphs

11. **(A)** Checkers is one of the most widely played board games in the world. Checkers was played in ancient Egypt and Greece. The game is played by two players. The goal is to capture all the opponent's pieces by jumping over them.
(B) Checkers is one of the most widely played board games in the world. It has been around since ancient Egypt and Greece and is easier to play and learn than other board games like chess. People of all ages enjoy checkers all around the world.

12. **(A)** Board games are fun, but they also sharpen mental skills. They often require logic and mathematical reasoning. Board games involve strategy and skill. Young children who play board games tend to do better in school. Parents would be wise to play a lot of board games with their young children.
(B) Board games are fun, but they also sharpen mental skills. Board games like chess, checkers, and backgammon are played all over the world. Many board games were played in ancient times. There are many computer versions of popular board games.

13. **(A)** Golf is a great sport that can be played well into old age. Golf Golf began in Scotland in the 1400s. The first golf course in the United States opened in 1888.
(B) Golf is a great sport that can be played well into old age. Professional golf includes both men's and women's professional tours, but millions of people play golf for fun. Once you learn how to play, you can play it your whole life.

14. **(A)** Both the Winter and Summer Olympics showcase the world's finest athletes. Starting in 1994, the winter and summer Olympic Games have been held two years apart instead of the same year. Winter sports include bobsled, ice hockey, figure skating, and snowboarding. Summer games include baseball, canoeing, swimming, gymnastics, and track and field.
(B) Both the Winter and Summer Olympics showcase the world's finest athletes. Male and female athletes from all over the world compete in over fifty different sports. The best of these set world records and set the goals for tomorrow's athletes.

Unit 18
Writing a Bibliography

A **bibliography** is a list of sources used in a research report or other piece of writing. It is usually placed at the end of the piece of writing. Each **citation**, or entry, in the bibliography identifies the name, author, title, publisher, date published, and sometimes the page numbers of the source.

- A bibliography is arranged in alphabetical order by author. If there is no author, alphabetize by title.
- If there are two authors, the first author's name is reversed (last name, first name), but the second author's name is not reversed.

Use the sample bibliography entries to answer the questions that follow.

BOOK

Author's last name, author's first name. *Title of Book.* City and state of publication: name of publisher, year of publication.
Mija, Sin. *The Book of Fossils.* New York, NY: Past Life Press, 2003.

MAGAZINE

Author's last name, author's first name. "Title of Article." *Title of Magazine*. volume number, issue number, date of publication, page numbers.
McCord, Heather and Suvina Lent. "New Fossil Discoveries Point to Earliest Life." *Rock and Science.* v. 61, n. 3, April 24, 2004, p. 10.

NEWSPAPER

Author's last name, author's first name. "Title of Article." *Title of Newspaper*. Volume number, issue number, date of publication, page number.
Jones, Justin. "Fossil Hunting at Alum Creek" *The Columbus Messenger.* v. 44, n. 65, February 21, 2002, p. B8.

Unit 18

Writing a Bibliography

ENCYCLOPEDIA

Author's last name, author's first name. "Title of Entry." *Title of Encyclopedia*. Edition or version. If no author given, begin with "Title of Entry."

"Fossils." *Just the Facts Encyclopedia*. 2004 ed.

WEB SITE

Author's last name, author's first name. "Title of Page." Sponsor. Date written or last update. Date accessed. <Electronic address>.

Wilmoth, Jennifer. "The History of Fossil Hunting" *Science World*. September 15, 2002. Accessed September 30, 2003. <http://www.fossilhunting.org/scienceworld.htm>.

1. What is the name of the organization that sponsored the Web site about fossil hunting?
   (A) *Just the Facts Encyclopedia*
   (B) *Science World*
   (C) *Fossils*
   (D) "Fossil Hunting at Alum Creek"

2. On what page of the newspaper can the fossil hunting article be found?
   (A) 65
   (B) B8
   (C) 10
   (D) 44

3. What is the name of the publication in which the article "New Fossil Discoveries Point to Earliest Life" can be found?
   (A) *The Columbus Messenger*
   (B) *Just the Facts Encyclopedia*
   (C) *Hockey World*
   (D) *Rock and Science*

4. Which entry lists two authors?
   (A) book
   (B) magazine
   (C) newspaper
   (D) Web site

Unit 18
Writing a Bibliography

Answer the following questions about writing a bibliography.

5. Which is the correct way to write a citation for a book?
   (A) Stern, Mandy and Frazier, Martin. *Communication: From Stone Tablets to Wireless*. New York, NY: Little Fish Books, 2004.
   (B) *Communication: From Stone Tablets to Wireless.* Stern, Mandy and Martin Frazier. New York, NY: Little Fish Books, 2004.
   (C) Stern, Mandy and Martin Frazier. *Communication: From Stone Tablets to Wireless*. Little Fish Books: New York, NY, 2004.
   (D) Stern, Mandy and Martin Frazier. *Communication: From Stone Tablets to Wireless*. New York, NY: Little Fish Books, 2004.

6. Which is the correct way to write a citation for a Web site?
   (A) Hernandez, Taylor. "American Inventions." Unknown. None. March 1, 2004. <http://www.mywebsites.com/inventions.htm>.
   (B) Hernandez, Taylor. "American Inventions." March 1, 2004. <http://www.mywebsites.com/inventions.htm>.
   (C) Hernandez, Taylor. "American Inventions." Unknown. March 1, 2004. Accessed January 7, 2005. <http://www.mywebsites.com/inventions.htm>.
   (D) "American Inventions." March 1, 2004. <http://www.mywebsites.com/inventions.htm>.

7. Which is the correct way to write a citation for a newspaper article?
   (A) Juniper, Dickie. "Wall Street Hails New Invention." *Springfield Post*. v. 120, n. 5, Jan. 5, 2004, p. C1.
   (B) Juniper, Dickie. *Springfield Post and Times*. "Wall Street Hails New Invention." v. 120, n. 5, Jan. 5, 2004, p. C1.
   (C) Juniper, Dickie. "Wall Street Hails New Invention." *Springfield Post and Times*. v. 120, n. 5, Jan. 5, 2004, p. C1.
   (D) Juniper, Dickie. "Wall Street Hails New Invention." *Springfield Post and Times*. v. 120, n. 5, Jan. 5, 2004.

8. Which is the correct way to write a citation for a Web site?

(A) Morris, Sharon. “Who’s Who of World Inventors.” Block School. March 7, 2004. Accessed September 15, 2004. <http://www.block.edu/gr4/invent.htm>.

(B) Morris, Sharon. 2004. “Who’s Who of World Inventors.” Block School. March 7, 2004. <http://www.block.edu/gr4/invent.htm>.

(C) Morris, Sharon. “Who’s Who of World Inventors.” 2004. Block School. March 7, 2004. <http://www.block.edu/gr4/invent.htm>.

(D) Morris, Sharon. “Who’s Who of World Inventors.” March 7, 2004. Block School. 2004. <http://www.block.edu/gr4/invent.htm>.

---

9. Which is the correct way to write a citation for a book?

(A) Owen Davis. *Twentieth-Century Inventions.* New York, NY: Lighthouse Books, 2003.

(B) Davis, Owen. *Twentieth-Century Inventions.* New York, NY: Lighthouse Books, 2003.

(C) Davis, Owen. *Twentieth-Century Inventions.* Lighthouse Books: New York, NY, 2003.

(D) *Twentieth-Century Inventions.* Davis, Owen. New York, NY: Lighthouse Books, 2003.

---

10. Which is the correct way to write a citation for a magazine article that has two authors?

(A) Boiler, Pam and Susan Kraybill. “The Century in Review: The Greatest Inventions of Our Time” *This Life*. v. 100, n. 12, December 2000, pp. 11–20.

(B) Boiler, Pam and Susan Kraybill. “The Century in Review: The Greatest Inventions of Our Time.” *This Life*. n. 12, v. 100, December 2000, pp. 11–20.

(C) Boiler, Pam and Kraybill, Susan. “The Century in Review: The Greatest Inventions of Our Time.” *This Life*. v. 100, n. 12, December 2000, pp. 11–20.

(D) Boiler, Pam and Susan Kraybill. “The Century in Review: The Greatest Inventions of Our Time.” December 2000, *This Life*. v. 100, n. 12, pp. 11–20.

The Last LAP

Language Activity Pages

A. Exercising Your Skill

You have been learning that the research process includes several steps. Answer each question below by choosing the stage in the research process that is described.

1. explain how you proved your thesis and why it is important
   (A) write an outline
   (B) take notes
   (C) write a concluding paragraph
2. create a loose guideline for your report
   (A) write an outline
   (B) write a bibliography
   (C) take notes
3. create a list of sources you used to write your report
   (A) make a research statement
   (B) write a bibliography
   (C) summarize information
4. provide a variety of evidence to prove your thesis
   (A) write a bibliography
   (B) write a concluding paragraph
   (C) write three supporting paragraphs

B. Expanding Your Skill

Choose the best outline for the research statement below.

1. Golf is the perfect sport.
   (A) I. Sports introduction
   A. Basketball
   B. Baseball
   C. Golf
   II. Golf conclusion
   (B) I. Benefits of Playing Golf
   A. Play golf your whole life
   B. Not a contact sport, so few injuries
   C. Walking and muscular coordination
   II. Golf conclusion

C. Exploring Language

Expository Writing Read the paragraph below. Choose the best summary for the paragraph.

Since Yellowstone National Park was created more than 125 years ago, 384 sites have become part of the national park system. Some of these sites are memorials to famous people, like Lincoln's Home in Springfield, Illinois. Others are monuments to a specific event, like the Battle of Gettysburg in Pennsylvania. Other sites preserve America's wildlife and diverse beauty, like Yellowstone itself. Without the national park system, America's cultural and natural heritage would be endangered.

(A) There are different kinds of national parks.
(B) The national park system, which includes 384 sites, plays a vital role in maintaining America's cultural and natural heritage.
(C) Lincoln's Home, Gettysburg, and Yellowstone are three different kinds of national parks.

D. Expressing Yourself

Choose one of these activities. When you are finished, give your paper to your teacher.

1. Complete the following steps for a report about a national park.
   a. Choose a topic.
   b. Write a research statement.
   c. Use at least three different resources to research your topic.
   d. Take notes.
   e. Summarize your research. Remember to paraphrase.
   f. Write an outline.
   g. Write an introductory paragraph.
   h. Write three supporting paragraphs.
   i. Write a concluding paragraph.
   j. Write a bibliography.
2. WORK with a PARTNER Find information about a national park in five different sources. Evaluate and compare the different types of information you found. Present your findings to the class.

RESEARCH Scope and Sequence • *Specific Skill Series for Language Arts*

Unit/Level	Level A	Level B	Level C	Level D	Level E	Level F	Level G	Level H
Unit 1	Parts of a Book	Using a Library	Using a Library	Using a Table of Contents	Using a Table of Contents and an Index	Getting Ideas and Narrowing a Topic	Getting Ideas and Narrowing a Topic	Getting Ideas and Narrowing a Topic
Unit 2	Using Books	Using a Table of Contents	Using a Table of Contents	Using an Index	Using an Encyclopedia	Formulating Questions	Formulating Questions	Formulating Questions
Unit 3	Using a Table of Contents	Using an Encyclopedia	Using an Index	Finding Magazine and Newspaper Articles	Finding Magazine and Newspaper Articles	Making a Research Statement	Making a Research Statement	Making a Research Statement
Unit 4	Using a Table of Contents	Key Word Searching	Using an Encyclopedia	Key Word Searching	Key Word Searching	Finding Information	Finding Information	Finding Information
Unit 5	Using an Encyclopedia	Evaluating a Web Site	Key Word Searching	Evaluating a Web Site	Evaluating a Web Site	Using a Table of Contents	Using an Atlas	Using an Atlas
Unit 6	Using an Encyclopedia	Reading a Chart	Evaluating a Web Site	Getting Ideas	Reading Graphs and Charts	Finding Newspaper and Magazine Articles	Finding Newspaper and Magazine Articles	Finding Newspaper and Magazine Articles
Unit 7	Reading a Chart	Taking a Survey	Reading a Chart	Asking Questions	Getting Ideas and Narrowing Your Topic	Key Word Searching	Key Word Searching	Key Word Searching
Unit 8	Taking a Survey	Reading a Diagram	Taking a Survey	Making a Research Statement	Formulating Questions	Evaluating Web Sites	Evaluating Web Sites	Evaluating Web Sites
Unit 9	Finding Information	Getting Ideas	Reading a Diagram	Finding Information	Making a Research Statement	Reading Graphs and Charts	Reading Graphs and Charts	Reading Graphs and Charts
Unit 10	Taking Notes	Asking Questions	Getting Ideas	Comparing Information across Sources	Identifying Sources	Comparing Information across Sources	Comparing Sources	Comparing Sources
Unit 11		Making a Research Statement	Asking Questions	Evaluating Information	Comparing Information across Sources	Taking Notes	Taking Notes	Taking Notes
Unit 12		Finding Information	Making a Research Statement	Taking Notes	Taking Notes	Summarizing	Summarizing	Summarizing
Unit 13		Taking Notes	Finding Information	Summarizing	Summarizing	Writing an Outline	Writing an Outline	Writing an Outline
Unit 14			Evaluating Information	Writing an Outline	Writing an Outline	Writing Introductory Paragraphs	Writing Introductory Paragraphs	Writing Introductory Paragraphs
Unit 15				Writing Paragraphs	Writing Introductory Paragraphs	Writing Supporting Paragraphs	Writing Supporting Paragraphs	Writing Supporting Paragraphs
Unit 16				Writing a Bibliography	Writing Supporting Paragraphs	In-Text Citations	In-Text Citations	In-Text Citations
Unit 17					Writing Concluding Paragraphs	Writing Concluding Paragraphs	Writing Concluding Paragraphs	Writing Concluding Paragraphs
Unit 18					Writing a Bibliography	Writing a Bibliography	Writing a Bibliography	Writing a Bibliography